Making a Difference

REDUCING

Garbage

Sue Barraclough

SEA-TO-SEA

Mankato Collingwood London

This edition first published in 2008 by
Sea-to-Sea Publications
1980 Lookout Drive
North Mankato
Minnesota 56003

Library of Congress
Cataloging in Publication Data:

Barraclough, Sue.
   Reducing garbage / by Sue Barraclough.
      p.cm. (Making a difference)
   Includes bibliographical references and index.
   ISBN 978-1-59771-110-4
   1. Waste minimization--Juvenile literature. I. Title.

TD793.9.B37 2007
363.72'82-dc22

                    2006060721

9 8 7 6 5 4 3

Published by arrangement with the Watts Publishing Group Ltd, London.

Original concept devised by
Sue Barraclough and Jemima Lumley.

Editor: Adrian Cole
Designer: Jemima Lumley
Art director: Jonathan Hair
Special photography: Mark Simmons
Consultant: Helen Peake, Education Officer at
  The Recycling Consortium, Bristol

Acknowledgments:
The author and publisher wish to thank Helen Peake and the staff at
The Recycling Consortium. Images on pages 7tc, 8, 13t, supplied by
the national Recycle Now campaign (for more information on recycling
visit www.recyclenow.com). Chris Fairclough; page 9. Ava, Connie,
James, Romi, Ruby, Vincent, and Tom for taking part.

Contents

What is reducing?

Reducing means to make less. We need to reduce our garbage, or rubbish.

Think before you throw things away, because many materials should not be thrown into the garbage can.

The materials below in the green sections should not be put into a garbage can. They can be reused or recycled. We can also reduce rubbish by not creating so much of it.

Vegetable and fruit waste

Metal cans

Paper

This packaging cannot be recycled

Glass

Why reduce garbage?

Most garbage that you put into the trash can is buried at a landfill site. We do not have enough room to continue burying huge amounts of garbage.

What you can do

Before you throw something away try to reuse it, or find someone else that can.

Garbage like this can cause pollution
to land, air, and water. It can be
dangerous for all living things.

Reducing packaging

Most of the things we buy are wrapped in packaging. Packaging is the box, the wrapping, or the bag that you buy something in.

Packets

Cartons

String

Boxes

Wrappers

Bags

Trays

Some packaging is useful because it stops food from getting squashed or broken. Other packaging is there only to make something look good. Most packaging is usually thrown away.

When you buy something from a store, think about the packaging. Is it made from recycled material? Can it be reused or recycled?

All this packaging is for a handful of beads! Some of the plastic could be reused and the cardboard can be recycled.

Take less garbage home

At the store you can help
choose things with less
packaging. Your family will have less
garbage to recycle or throw away.

Help choose loose vegetables and fruit. Lots of food has a plastic wrapper and tray that have to be thrown away.

What you can do

Some stores sell food without packaging. You can scoop out what you need. Avoid boxes and cartons if you can.

Think about garbage

Think about garbage when you go to a store. Look for things that have too much packaging.

Shopping tips to reduce garbage:

Make a shopping list so you do not buy things you do not need.

Take bags with you to the store. Then you can say, "No, thank you." to plastic and paper bags.

Buy cans of pet food, not packets. The foil packages have to be thrown away. The cans can be recycled.

Buy big bottles of juice. Using one big bottle, instead of two or three smaller ones, cuts down on garbage.

Avoid plastic packaging. Choose items with packaging made of paper or glass. These can be recycled easily.

No-garbage lunchbox

If you have take your lunch to school with you, use a lunchbox with sections. Then you do not have to wrap anything up in packaging.

Drink carton

Metal foil

Plastic wrapping

What you can do

At home, wash out your empty lunchbox and get it ready. What things could you put in it that do not have lots of packaging?

Refills reduce garbage

Think of all the bottles and cartons that get put in the garbage can every day.

If you refill and reuse bottles you can reduce your rubbish.

Make a simple funnel using half an old plastic bottle. This makes refilling bottles much easier.

What you can do

Use a plastic bottle that can be refilled. If you take a bottle to school every day you will save five bottles or cartons in one week.

Make your own

If you make and bake your own food, you can cut down on some packaging.

Most food and take-out packaging has to be thrown away.

Pizzas are easy and quick to make. See page 27 for a simple pizza recipe.

Making food is fun. Just think about all the packaging you won't have to throw away.

Grow your own food

Another good way to
reduce rubbish is to grow
your own food. You can
use old packaging as
seed trays.

Seeds

Look for seeds in
different fruits and
vegetables.

You can buy packages
of seeds to grow your
favorite vegetables.

Cress

**What
you can do**

Try growing
cress seeds.
Just sprinkle them
on wet tissue.

Sorting out garbage

When you have finished with
something, do not just throw it
into a garbage can. Sort out and
save glass, paper, and metal
for reusing or recycling.

**A can
crusher**

Ask an adult to help you crush
cans. They will take up less room
in your recycling box.

Put vegetable and fruit waste
into a compost bin or wormery.

Sort out recycling into
storage boxes. It will
be easy to empty them
on collection day.

Glass

Metal

Paper

All sorts of packaging

Can you guess what was in this packaging? How could you reuse it?

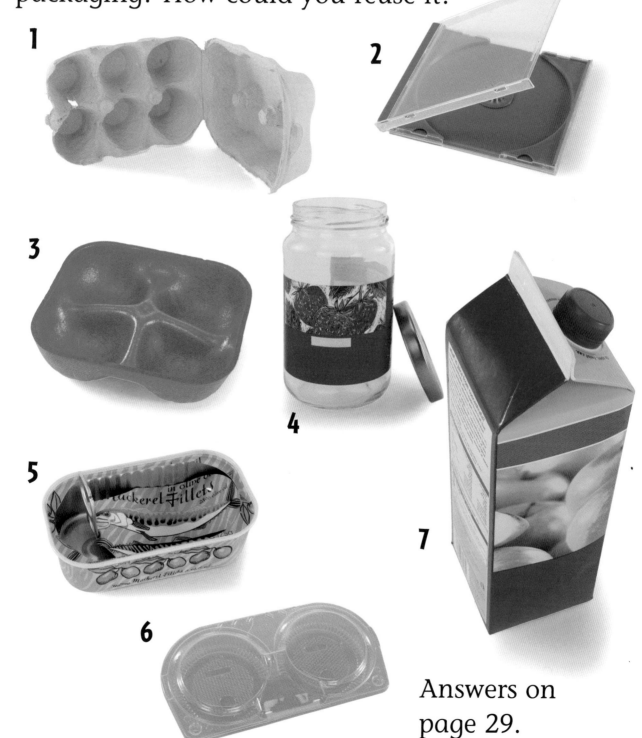

1

2

3

4

5

6

7

Answers on page 29.

Make a pizza

It is easy to make your own pizza.
You can choose your own topping.
You won't have lots of packaging left over.

You will need:
• A pizza-base mix.
(You could use some thick
slices of bread instead).
• Tomato paste.
• Cheese.
• Different toppings, such
as peppers and mushrooms.

1. Ask an adult to preheat the oven to 425°F/220°C.

2. Use a pizza base mix to make your pizza base.

3. Now spread over some tomato paste.

4. Next, cover with your toppings.
We chose peppers and slices of cheese.

5. Sprinkle some grated cheese on top.

6. Finally, ask an adult to bake your pizza
in the oven for 20–25 minutes.

Find out more

Reducing garbage is all about rethinking rubbish. Some packaging protects our food and keeps it fresh, but a lot of packaging is not really needed. You can help reduce garbage by avoiding packaging that cannot be recycled or reused.
Try not to buy products that have too much packaging.

www.factmonster.com
Type "recycling" in the search box to find lots of useful links and recycling information.

www.eia.doe.gov/kids/ energyfacts/saving/recycling
The U.S. Government Energy Information Administration's site for children has comprehensive information about all aspects of recycling paper and glass.

www.kid-at-art.com
This website tells you all about creative ways to recycle by making art.

www.earth911.org/ master.asp
Click on the "Kids" link for educational children's activities and information on every aspect of recycling.

www.metrokc.gov/dnr/ kidsweb
Games and information on sorting rubbish and the 3Rs (Reducing, Reusing, and Recycling).

Every effort has been made by the Publisher to ensure that these websites contain no inappropriate or offensive material. However, because of the nature of the Internet, it is impossible to guarantee that the contents of these sites will not be altered. We strongly advise that Internet access is supervised by a responsible adult.

Glossary

Compost bin—a container used to store kitchen and garden waste where it breaks down.

Landfill site—a huge hole in the ground that is filled with garbage.

Material—the substance something is made from. For example, paper is made from a material called wood.

Packaging—bottles, jars, cartons, boxes, bags, wrappings, and containers. All these things can be made from materials such as paper, glass, and plastic.

Pollution—making something dirty or poisoning it.

Recycle—using something again or make it into something new.

Recycling collection scheme—a system where materials to be recycled are picked up from the curbside.

Seeds—the parts of a plant that can grow into new plants.

Wormery—a special container to hold worms and waste. The waste is eaten by the worms.

Answers to the quiz on page 26: 1—eggs, use to store coins, etc; 2—a CD, use to keep computer disks in; 3—fruit, use as a paint-mixing palette; 4—strawberry jam, use as a pencil jar; 5—fish, recycle; 6—cakes, fill with water and seed to feed birds outside; 7—apple juice, some cartons cannot be recycled or reused.

Index

About this book

Making A Difference: Reducing Garbage encourages children to think about the problems of throwing away lots of garbage, especially packaging.

The book introduces a range of first-hand experiences that children can use to extend their knowledge and understanding of the world. The opening pages focus on the idea that many of the things we throw in the trash can be recycled.

Pages 8 and **9** explore why it is important to reduce waste. Discuss the idea that all the garbage we throw away will be burned or buried.
Use **pages 10** and **11** to think about packaging, and then use pages **12–15** to think about different ideas to reduce rubbish while you shop.
Pages 16–17 explore the ideal of having no garbage at all to throw-away, with a no-garbage lunchbox.

Pages 18–23 look at some practical ideas and projects for reducing garbage.
Pages 24–28 take a look at simple ways to sort out garbage, and how children can get involved.

These simple ideas can form the foundations of thinking about our impact on the planet, saving natural resources, and whether we are living sustainably.

SANTA FE PUBLIC LIBRARY